Tough
TRUCKS

To Billy, Arthur, Sophie, Guy, and Jan—T. M.
For Frank—A. P.

The Publisher thanks the Road Haulage Association in the U.K., the Chicago Department of Streets and Sanitation, and the National Truck Equipment Association in the U.S. for their kind assistance in the development of this book.

KINGFISHER
LONDON & NEW YORK

Distributed in the U.S. by Macmillan, 175 Fifth Ave., New York, NY 10010
Distributed in Canada by H.B. Fenn and Company Ltd.,
34 Nixon Road, Bolton, Ontario L7E 1W2

Library of Congress Cataloging-in-Publication Data
has been applied for.

ISBN: 978-0-7534-5917-1

Kingfisher books are available for special promotions and premiums.
For details contact: Special Markets Department,
Macmillan, 175 Fifth Ave., New York, NY 10010.

For more information, please visit www.kingfisherbooks.com

Printed in China
10 9 8 7 6 5

Tough
TRUCKS

Tony Mitton and
Ant Parker

KINGFISHER
NEW YORK

rumble

Trucks are tough and sturdy.
They take on heavy loads,

rumble

then thunder on their giant tires
down long and busy roads.

All trucks have a cab up front.
The driver sits inside.
The truck's controls are all around,
ready for the ride.

The driver starts the engine
and, when the way is clear,
accelerates along the road
and turns the wheel to steer.

Some truck cabs have a bunk bed,
a curtain, and a light

to make a tiny bedroom
where the driver sleeps at night.

A big rig has a semitrailer
fitted with a pin.
Its tractor unit has a slot
to click the trailer in.

So when the rig is traveling
on roads that weave and wend,
the separate parts turn one by one
to get around a bend.

A garbage truck collects the trash,
grumbling down the street.

It lifts the cans and empties them
to keep things clean and neat.

A concrete mixer stirs its load
while traveling to the site.
The foreman points, "Just pour it here.
We're ready now. All right?"

This shiny tanker's full of milk,
all creamy, cool, and white.

When traveling long distances,
you're on the road alone,
so drivers keep in touch
by CB radio or phone.

This truck has had a breakdown,
but the driver didn't panic.
He radioed around and found
a handy truck mechanic.

Driving trucks is tiring,
but you need to be awake.

So drivers park at truck stops
for a meal or a break.

But look, we've reached the depot.
We've made another run.

The forklift starts unloading,
and the foreman shouts, "Well done!"

Truck parts

tractor-trailer

this is made up of a tractor and a semitrailer—
it is also called a **semi** or a **big rig**

cab

this is where the driver sits

↑ semitrailer

this holds the truck's load

↑ tractor

this pulls the trailer

CB radio

a driver can use this special
radio to talk to other drivers

piston

also called a **hoist**, this is
a strong pump that pushes
up the back of a dump
truck to help it tip
its load